TREVOR HUDSON

# Pauses
# *for* Advent

——

## Words of Wonder

UPPER
ROOM BOOKS®
NASHVILLE

Upper Room Books® website: upperroombooks.com

Upper Room®, Upper Room Books®, and design logos are trademarks owned by The Upper Room®, Nashville, Tennessee. All rights reserved.

Scripture quotations not otherwise noted are from the New Revised Standard Version Bible, copyright 1989 National Council of the Churches of Christ in the United States of America. Used by permission. All rights reserved.

Cover design, illustration, and interior design: Faceout Studio
Cover image:: Shutterstock

Library of Congress Cataloging-in-Publication Data

Names: Hudson, Trevor, 1951– author.
Title: Pauses for Advent : words of wonder / Trevor Hudson.
Description: Nashville : Upper Room Books, 2017. |
Identifiers: LCCN 2016056669 (print) | LCCN 2017027255 (ebook) | ISBN 9780835817110 (Mobi) | ISBN 9780835817127 (Epub) | ISBN 9780835817103 (print)
Subjects: LCSH: Advent—Meditations.
Classification: LCC BV40 (ebook) | LCC BV40 .H83 2017 (print) | DDC 242/.332—dc23
LC record available at https://lccn.loc.gov/2016056669

Printed in the United States of America

# Contents

## Fourth Week of Advent

# INTRODUCTION

After almost forty years in pastoral ministry, I have noticed a few things about how people experience Christmas. On one hand, they yearn to celebrate the mystery of the season in a way that is meaningful, significant, and even transformative. On the other hand, they reach Christmas Day feeling unprepared and unready. Shopping, finalizing holiday plans to visit friends and family, and decorating their homes gobble up the days preceding Christmas and fill them with anxiety. Christmas Day arrives, and they have not observed Advent the way they intended. Consequently, their celebration of the Christ child on Christmas Day lacks a sense of wonder.

In this little book, I want to respond to the widespread yearning for a more wondrous experience of Christmas. The Christian calendar is shaped by different seasons. These seasons are "time gifts" that the church gives us to participate more deeply in what God has done and is doing in the world. Beginning with Advent (the start of the Christian year), we receive the opportunity to enter into the mystery of Jesus' birth. Lent, a season consisting of forty days, prepares us to participate in the death and resurrection of Jesus. Ascension reminds us that Christ's presence fills the universe, while Pentecost invites us to open our lives to the presence of the Holy Spirit. Each season represents a vital part God's story. Each one needs to be observed thoughtfully, deliberately, and intentionally. When we don't, our spiritual journey becomes impoverished, lopsided, and one-dimensional.

So how can we fill the season of Advent with more wonder? As Tom Wright, the distinguished New Testament scholar, reminds us, if we remove Advent—that is, attentively waiting for Jesus' birth—from the Bible, we lose half the Old Testament and most of the New, including stories of Jesus' ancestors, the words of the prophets, and the mystery of the Incarnation. Most certainly, if we don't observe Advent thoughtfully, we will not arrive at Christmas ready for the Christ child. We will come to that special day not too sure what the fuss is all about. But if we embrace Advent—this special time of anticipating the mystery of the Incarnation—we will find our celebration of Jesus' coming at Bethlehem filled with wonder and awe.

What is Advent all about? Built around the four Sundays leading up to Christmas Day, Advent provides us with time for preparation. We seek to prepare for the coming of Jesus—who has come in the past, who continually comes in the present, and who will come in the future. During Advent, we pray with our heart and mind, *Come, Lord Jesus, come.* Along with this prayer of deep longing and yearning, we wait and watch, we remember and repent, we believe and behold. Above all, we seek to stay awake and become aware. Jesus often enters our lives in quiet, hidden, and unexpected ways.

How can we go about taking Advent more seriously? I have a few suggestions. First, let's pause briefly each day during the four weeks of Advent. When a dear friend heard that I was writing about pausing for Advent, she sent me the sage words of self-help writer and counselor Hugh Prather: "Life is lived in the pauses, not the events." So how can we be intentional about pausing each day? We can select a period of time between five and ten minutes when we can be alone and uninterrupted. We can set aside this time by creating a reminder in our smartphone or calendar, deciding on a place where we can go, and making the commitment to be faithful to this time during Advent.

Second, we can read each day's brief reflection, which includes a themed meditation based on a biblical word and a passage from scripture. Reading these reflections should not take more than a few minutes. These words will illuminate the different themes of Advent preparation: waiting, watching, remembering, repenting, believing, and beholding. We can take each word with us into the rest of our day and allow it to percolate within our heart and mind. What might God be saying to us through the word? How can we interact with this word given the events and encounters of our own life?

On the Sundays of Advent, I offer longer meditations, focusing on the people who witnessed Jesus' birth and came to celebrate the Messiah. We meet these persons each year, meaning their stories sometimes become stale and redundant in our minds—*Oh, I've heard this one before*, we think. Instead of relating their stories to our own life, we let these men and women remain merely characters in a somewhat foreign and faraway land from a story we've heard many times over. This Advent, let's ask ourselves what can we learn from their attitudes and actions that we can apply to our own life, opening ourselves to a more profound experience of the Christmas mystery.

Third, each day I provide a simple daily practice. Thoughts alone seldom transform us; we also must act with intention. This belief led me to suggesting a particular action that embodies the word we are contemplating. The daily practice may be something we have never done before or something we do every day. Regardless, I hope we approach it with awareness and intentionality. Through reflecting and then acting, we will become "contemplatives in action."

Finally, this Advent journey can be made with a friend or a small group of fellow pilgrims. Those reading this book with a group will want to meet once a week to discuss and share their experience of the words and practices. This group meeting is not a time to teach, preach, fix, or advise; instead, I encourage participants to simply share and listen. Finding words to describe our experiences and listening to the experiences of others grows us in our discipleship. We create our own personal stories of faith by sharing with others what God is doing in our lives and by learning from what God may be doing in the lives of those around us.

So, dear readers, may we experience a blessed Advent and Christmas season. I hope these words and practices will deepen our experience of the Christ child so that he may be born in us afresh. May we allow Jesus to enter our heart, mind, and soul so that he may become visible to others through who we are, what we say, and what we do. When this happens, we have truly prepared ourselves for the wonder of Christmas!

# PREPARE

### Read Isaiah 40:1-8.

*A voice cries out:*
*"In the wilderness prepare the way of the L*ORD.*"*
**Isaiah 40:3**

Advent is all about preparing ourselves for the coming Messiah, who has already come in the past, continually comes to us in the here and now, and will come again in the future. The question we ask today is this: How do we prepare ourselves so that he can come into our lives, into our relationships, and into the fractured and broken world where we live?

In Isaiah 40, we find three preparation hints. First, we prepare by clearing a straight path through the wilderness. The wilderness is a lonely place. We are surrounded today by so many people living in loneliness. Often, the Christmas season accentuates that loneliness. Connecting with a lonely person can open a pathway for Jesus to touch his or her life. Or, when we find ourselves feeling lonely, we can risk connecting with someone who may help us meet Jesus anew.

Second, we prepare by leveling the mountains and the valleys. Mountains and valleys symbolize those barriers that make us feel as though we are separated from Jesus. For example, such barriers may be hunger, poverty, unemployment, or mental health issues. Engaging these obstacles for ourselves and on behalf of others can prepare the way for Jesus to come to those who struggle.

Third, we prepare by remembering we are like grass. Grass symbolizes our fragility, our vulnerability, and our weakness. We spend so much of our lives running from this reality, and we often miss the grace, mercy, and steadfastness of Jesus, who is strength in our weakness. Embracing the reality of our frailty opens up possibilities for encountering the living Christ.

Advent holds before us the challenge of preparation. Are we interested enough in Jesus who makes our paths straight through the wilderness, who levels the mountains and they valleys of our lives, and who reminds us that his Word will stand forever?

### *Daily Practice*

Make one phone call to someone who is feeling lonely or struggling. Let him or her know that he or she is in your thoughts. Ask how you can serve him or her. Keep him or her close to your heart in prayer today.

# OPEN

## Read Revelation 3:15-22.

*"Listen! I am standing at the door, knocking;*
*if you hear my voice and open the door,*
*I will come in to you and eat with you, and you with me."*
**Revelation 3:20**

In the famous painting by William Holman Hunt of this scene from Revelation called "The Light of the World," Jesus is standing with a lamp in his hand, knocking on a closed door with no handle on the outside. The door must be opened from the inside.

Advent is a time for us to open the door of our life to Jesus. He is not going to force his way in. He wants to have a genuine friendship with us—not a forced relationship. We have little chance of Jesus freely coming to live in us and we living in him without this freedom. God took the immense risk of creating human beings with free will who can resist the divine love offered to them. We are free to open the door of our heart or to keep it shut.

Sometimes we want to keep the door to our heart closed because of the mess inside. Few things keep the door closed more tightly than shame and guilt. When we make a mistake, we often close ourselves off from God, from life, and from others. We punish ourselves, believing that we are bad and that God wants nothing to do with us. However, this does not stop Jesus from knocking on our door, wanting to enter and be with us.

Even after we have opened the door of our heart to Jesus, we still may be tempted to keep some interior rooms locked. We keep other doors closed because we ourselves are scared of facing the darkness or chaos there. Our Advent invitation today could be opening the front door of our heart to Jesus or opening the doors of other rooms and entering with Jesus by our side. In this way, we allow the light and joy of Christmas to fill the dark and hidden places of our lives.

### *Daily Practice*

Exercise your imagination today. Imagine sitting in your favorite room alone and with the door closed. Imagine hearing a knock at the door. Open the door, and imagine Jesus standing in the doorway. What does he say to you? What do you say to him?

# GUARD

## Read Luke 21:34-36.

*"Be on guard so that your hearts are not weighed down with dissipation and drunkenness and the worries of this life, and that day does not catch you unexpectedly."*
**Luke 21:34**

The challenge of Advent is clear: How do we prepare for the Lord's coming? In the Gospel of Luke, we find these words: "Be on guard." In the verse above, Jesus refers to those actions that dull our sensitivity to the divine presence in our lives. These obstacles range from drunkenness to anxieties about what we have and don't have. Certainly these are not the only habits that undermine our awareness of the Lord's coming, but Jesus notices these issues in the people of his day, and his words are certainly relevant for us as well.

The Christmas season often becomes a time when excessive partying and drinking is the order of the day. Many companies plan a Christmas party for their employees. We want to share in these festive moments, have fun with colleagues, and relax with those with whom we work. Yet, the temptation to drink excessively is all too real. The intoxicated mind becomes tragically blurred to the mystery of the coming Christ child and keeps us from fully seeing his wonder and glory. Being on guard keeps us from falling into this trap while we are having a good time.

Another intoxication that obscures Jesus in our midst is our consumerism. Sadly, the Advent season sees many of us succumb to what Walter Burghardt, SJ, simply calls the "consumer bug."

We see something; we like it; we buy it. When we no longer like it, we throw it away and buy it again—this time perhaps more expensively. We overconsume in a world where others don't have enough. Few of us can plead innocence in this regard. Being a consumer can consume us. To be on guard means we remain vigilant every time we enter a shopping mall and walk down its corridors.

Today, we have focused on two possible intruders that can blur our recognition of the Lord's coming, but there are many others. Thankfully, we can look to scripture for a way to keep our vision clear: Be on guard.

### *Daily Practice*

Declare today a no-drinking and no-shopping day. Allow your fast to deepen your awareness of the presence of the living God all around you, especially in the lives of those who are in need this season.

# AWAKE

## Read Mark 13:32-37.

*"What I say to you I say to all: Keep awake."*
**Mark 13:37**

How easily we succumb to sleepwalking through our lives. We go from experience to experience, encounter to encounter, event to event on autopilot, showing little awareness that Jesus is present and active in our midst. Consequently, we confine our life of faith to certain religious moments such as going to church, saying our prayers, or offering grace before a meal, and our everyday existence gets divorced from our spiritual life. Sleepwalking endangers our spiritual health.

Advent is a time to wake up. To awaken is to live in a constant state of awareness and attentiveness so that we do not miss Jesus, who is ever-present and ever-active. It means living in the expectancy that we may be surprised by grace and mercy breaking into our lives at any moment. The ordinary things are not to be taken for granted; rather, they are the places, as Rowan Williams, the former archbishop of Canterbury, has pointed out, where we always can expect something new from our Master and Teacher that will touch our lives in some way. If we are sleeping, we may miss these Advent gifts!

So how do we wake up? A few simple practices come to mind. We can choose to receive each new day with gratitude and joy, to appreciate our early morning cup of coffee, to open our eyes to whatever is before us, to listen carefully to what is being said by those we are with, to taste the food we are eating, to give our attention fully to whatever task we are completing, to take time to appreciate the sounds and sensations around us, and to focus our attention on the present moment. And in whatever we do, we seek to be expectant—expectant that the Messiah who has come will come again and meet us in the here and now. Being awake is all about experiencing Jesus wherever we are, in whatever we are doing, with whomever we find ourselves.

### *Daily Practice*

Before going to bed tonight, think back over your day. Recall a moment when you were fully awake to the world around you. Then, remember a moment through which you sleepwalked. Notice the difference between these two moments, and ask God to help you stay awake throughout your day tomorrow.

# WREATH

### Read 1 Corinthians 9:24-25.

*Athletes exercise self-control in all things;*
*they do it to receive a perishable wreath,*
*but we an imperishable one.*
### 1 Corinthians 9:25

On the Sundays leading up to Christmas Day, church members often place an Advent wreath at the front of the church. This wreath contains five candles—four candles, which represent the four weeks of Advent, and one Christ candle, which represents the Light of the world. Each week, the service may open with someone lighting the appropriate candle and singing an Advent hymn. The mood of this worship moment is usually joyful, expectant, and filled with anticipation.

The Advent wreath serves as more than seasonal decoration. It carries both a hopeful meaning and a powerful challenge. To explain its meaning, Paul draws a helpful analogy in First Corinthians. Serious athletes, he points out, enter competitions in order to win a wreath or prize that gathers dust and may eventually be thrown away. In contrast, God promises an eternal and everlasting wreath to those Christ followers who remain faithful to the end. They will inherit a deathless, incorruptible, and glorious body in God's new heaven and earth.

The challenge of the wreath follows this promise. To become the people God wants us to be, we need to employ a strict training regimen, just like successful athletes do. This training will require us to engage in activities that grow our discipleship, such as study, worship, confession, service, and prayer. This training may also mean abstaining from our normal desires for food, conversation, company, and comfort for certain periods of time through the disciplines of fasting, silence, solitude, simplicity, and sacrifice. Without actually practicing spiritual exercises, we will not experience the joyful fulfillment that comes from being Christ followers.

During Advent, we both celebrate God's promise of an eternal future and consider how best we can train for our discipleship. This is the message that the Advent wreath proclaims.

### *Daily Practice*

Experiment briefly today either with one of the disciplines of engagement or with one of the disciplines of abstinence. You may choose to include this particular practice with your other spiritual practices for the rest of Advent.

# KEY

## Read Isaiah 22:20-22.

*I will place on his shoulder the key of the house of David;*
*he shall open, and no one shall shut;*
*he shall shut, and no one shall open.*
**Isaiah 22:22**

A key is a powerful symbol. Think for a moment about what it means to possess the key to a house. We can lock or open the door; we can come and go whenever we please; we have the power to grant or refuse someone's entrance.

In today's reading, God promises the key to Eliakim. In Jewish history, Eliakim was known as a caring father to the people of Israel. Intriguingly, within the Advent worship liturgy of the ancient church, Eliakim came to be seen as an image of the coming Messiah. In the New Testament, we learn that Jesus is the key of David who opens all our closed doors. (See Revelation 3:7.) Not only does he have the key to open the door for us into the heart and life of God, but also he has the key to open our hearts for the Spirit to come and live in us. This new two-way access is what Jesus comes to make possible.

Sometimes we feel as though we no longer have the key that lets us experience God and the Holy Spirit. This can be a painful, desolate, and frightening experience. Or perhaps we have been trying to use other keys to make sense of God and our lives, but they haven't worked. We long to experience God in a firsthand way, but we do not know where to turn. We yearn to know the warm companionship of the Spirit in our hearts but somehow feel orphaned and alone. In these moments, we need to discover again (or perhaps for the first time) that Jesus is the key we most deeply need. He is the key who grants us access to God and the Holy Spirit in deep, personal ways.

### *Daily Practice*

Each time you use a key today—to open the door of your home, to start your car, or to enter your office—remind yourself of what Jesus makes possible.

# MARY

## Read Luke 1:26-38.

*The angel said to [Mary], "The Holy Spirit will come upon you."*
**Luke 1:35**

Mary symbolizes a life into which Jesus is born. In the New Testament, she is the first Christ-bearer. Jesus is conceived in her womb. In her body, he is formed, and through her life, he comes into the world. Unlike Mary, we do not literally carry the flesh and blood of Jesus within us; even so, we are invited to bear his Spirit and share his presence with the world.

The Spirit of God allows Jesus' glorious presence to shine through us. Mary responds to the news that she will bear a son by asking Gabriel, "How can this be, since I am a virgin?" (Luke 1:34). The answer from God's messenger is clear: "The Holy Spirit will come upon you" (Luke 1:35). In other words—and as Mary discovers for herself—we do not become filled with Jesus' presence by our own efforts alone. God's Spirit fills us with Jesus' presence.

Still, this miracle requires our consent, which we see in Mary's response: "Let it be with me according to your word" (Luke 1:38). With these words, Mary says yes to God. She does so freely, humbly, and wholeheartedly. If we want Jesus to be born in our lives, we must offer ourselves to God each day. We must continually yield ourselves to God so that Jesus' love and grace may grow and deepen within us. God never forces the divine presence upon us; instead, God waits for our freely given yes.

Additionally, our yes to God inevitably leads to the loving service of others. Again, we see this reflected in Mary's encounter with Gabriel. She says, "Here am I, the servant of the Lord" (Luke 1:38). As we seek to love those around us this Christmas season, they will see the loving Light of the world shining through us. Our actions of love needn't be grand. We can simply show love whenever the opportunity arises, perhaps through a greeting, a smile, a thoughtful email, a phone call, a visit, a shared meal, or a listening ear. All these small and beautiful gifts of love express our desire to be God's servants wherever we are.

Let's allow our hearts to become Bethlehem this Advent. Although Jesus was born more than two thousand years ago, he wants to be born again in us today. Mary serves as our guide through this glorious and mysterious birth. When we open our hearts to the power of the Holy Spirit, when we consent to God's action within us, and when we become a conduit of divine love to all those we meet, Jesus is born again in and through us for the healing of the world.

### *Daily Practice*

Find a space today where you can spend five minutes with God. Sit comfortably with your eyes closed, place your open hands on your lap, and quiet your mind. Make Mary's words, "Let it be with me according to your word," your own prayer, and offer them to God along with the longings of your own heart. Should your attention wander, return ever so gently to Mary's words of self-offering and consecration.

# ANGEL

### Read Luke 2:8-9.

*An angel of the Lord stood before [the shepherds],*
*and the glory of the Lord shone around them,*
*and they were terrified.*
### Luke 2:9

Most of the people involved in the birth story of Jesus are surprised by an encounter with a messenger from God. Angels visit Mary, Joseph, Zechariah, and the shepherds, bringing special assurances of God's love and care for them. I can't imagine the Christmas story without angels; it would lose its mystery, light, and wonder.

The presence of angels reminds us that a reality exists beyond what we can see. Most of us have been educated in a worldview that only teaches about the physical realm. Within this space-time box, only those things that we can see and touch and measure are real. Advent invites us to see more widely than this and introduces us to another reality—the spiritual world that surrounds and penetrates the physical world. In this spiritual world, God is the most glorious and overwhelming inhabitant. We live and move and have our being immersed in these great invisibilities of the kingdom of God.

This Advent, may we be open to surprise visits from angels. Often they come in the guise of an unexpected stranger, an uninvited guest, or a chance encounter. In the letter to the Hebrews, the writer reminds us that when we show hospitality in these kinds of situations, we may entertain angels without knowing it. (See Hebrews 13:2.) Perhaps these angels will share messages similar to what Mary, Joseph, and Zechariah heard, or perhaps they will share the words of Jesus: "Do not be afraid. Let Christ be born in you. Allow divine love to flow through your life. Take care of the alien, the foreigner, and the exile in your land. Forgive and be reconciled."

Whatever messages the angels bring, we do not need to be afraid. Even if obeying the messages stretches us beyond the familiar and known, we can be sure that Emmanuel is with us.

### *Daily Practice*

Be open to God's surprises throughout the day. Say to the Lord, "I will watch for angels in all my encounters and heed your message as best I can."

# SHINE

### Read 2 Corinthians 4:5-6.

*It is the God who said, "Let light shine out of darkness,"*
*who has shone in our hearts to give the light of the knowledge*
*of the glory of God in the face of Jesus Christ.*
**2 Corinthians 4:6**

I have noticed that some people's faces seem to shine from within. Something about them is beautifully transparent and gloriously luminous with love. I am convinced that this "something" can only be the radiant goodness of God shining through them. Perhaps we all know such people.

Let's now imagine the blazing brightness that shines from Jesus' face. Wherever he goes, his life brings light to those who walk in darkness. He lights up the dark lives of those he touches with the light of God. His compassionate presence radiates at all times, even in the terrible darkness of the cross. His shining life was and is and always will be a reflection of the One who sent him.

In our dark world today, our hearts can easily become gloomy with despair and hopelessness. Before we even know what is happening, we may begin to reflect the darkness that surrounds us if our words and our actions come from a place of desolation rather than consolation. People look at our faces, and they no longer see the goodness and love of God shining through us. The light has gone out in our eyes. Our lives do not shine with compassion and warmth.

Advent invites us to open our hearts and minds to the eternal light of God. This could be one reason why we light candles during the season—not because we believe in candles but because we deeply desire to welcome the Light, which darkness can never overcome, and let it shine through our lives.

### *Daily Practice*

Take a few minutes today to sit in a darkened room. Consider those people in your life and in the world who may be living in darkness. Then, light a candle and pray that the light of God will shine through your life and into the lives of others.

# COMPASSION

**Read Luke 15:11-20.**

*"While [the younger son] was still far off,*
*his father saw him and was filled with compassion;*
*he ran and put his arms around him and kissed him."*
**Luke 15:20**

The word *compassion* evokes mixed feelings. We want to be known as compassionate people. As Christians, we believe that to be human is to be compassionate and to be compassionate is to be human. But when it comes to acting with compassion in the real world, we don't always hit the mark.

The God revealed to us in Jesus is compassionate through and through. Reread Jesus' words describing the father of the prodigal son. The father's whole being is permeated with compassion: his looking eyes, his overflowing heart, his running feet, his embracing arms, and his kissing lips. The litmus test for understanding our role as Christians is whether our lives reflect this radical compassion. If we want to know what God is like, we always look toward Jesus—and he embodies the meaning of *compassion*.

In a world overwhelmed with human suffering and pain, Jesus calls us to practice compassion. *Compassion* means "to suffer with." God relates to us in our suffering and invites us to be with others in theirs. However, we cannot offer to the hurting people around us what we have not ourselves received. Because of our struggles with self-rejection, guilt, and shame, receiving God's compassion can be difficult. When we find ourselves unable to accept God's compassion, we can pray to God for the ability to see ourselves the way God sees us.

So let us contemplate the God who comes to us in Jesus, open our hearts to receive divine compassion, and then work to make this compassion available to others.

### *Daily Practice*

Think of one person today to whom you can show compassion. Don't worry about what you will say or do. Remember that the greatest gift you can give someone in pain is your loving presence.

# WELCOME

## Romans 15:7-13.

*Welcome one another, therefore, just as Christ has welcomed you,*
*for the glory of God.*
**Romans 15:7**

To genuinely welcome people is to invite them into our space, to open our hearts to theirs, and to make them feel that they can be themselves in our presence. What a wonderful gift to offer others!

As our reading reminds us, Jesus offers us the gift of welcome. As the true Messiah, he fulfills the promise that God made to Abraham, Isaac, and Jacob. Through Jesus, God allows everyone and anyone to be welcomed into God's family.

Paul encourages us to offer the gospel-gift of welcome to others. Welcoming others can begin with a simple smile or an act of kindness. When someone in need crosses our path, we can be attentive, we can listen, and we can respond out of compassion and love instead of making him or her feel like an interruption or an imposition on our time. This is not easy, especially when the person we seek to welcome is vulnerable, in distress, or desperate for what we may find difficult to give.

But what does welcome have to do with Advent? Simply put, Jesus—the person we want to welcome into our hearts during this season—often comes to us disguised as a stranger. If this is true, as Jesus himself says it is, then we no longer can define Advent as four calendar weeks that we celebrate once a year. We celebrate Advent every time we welcome someone in Jesus' name and on his behalf, every time we look beyond ourselves and notice someone in need of love and compassion. Welcoming others involves becoming aware of people outside our families, our circle of friends, and our faith communities. We take a risk by reaching out, introducing ourselves, and taking an interest in their lives. May we remind ourselves today that welcoming the stranger is a gift of genuine Christmas love that we can give every day of the year.

### *Daily Practice*

Today, intentionally seek to be welcoming. Keep your office door open or invite someone you don't know to lunch. Offer a friendly smile to the cashier at the grocery store or visit neighbors who just moved in next door.

# WAIT

**Read Psalm 27:13-14.**

*Wait for the LORD;*
*be strong, and let you heart take courage;*
*wait for the LORD!*
**Psalm 27:14**

We often hear pastors say that Advent is all about waiting. But many people find that statement puzzling. After all, how do we wait for someone who has already come? Didn't Jesus come to us at Bethlehem? Didn't he also—after his resurrection and ascension—remain with us in his Spirit? What does it mean, then, to wait for someone who is with us right now?

Theologian Walter Burghardt, SJ, suggests that Mary helps us solve this puzzle. From the moment the angel leaves her, she knows that Jesus lives inside her. But she still has to wait. He is there, and yet he is still not there. Eventually, after months of active waiting and of preparing for his coming, Jesus is born to her and placed in a manger. He is who Mary has been waiting for. He comes to her from within her. Like Mary, we wait for Jesus who is already present within and around us to be birthed into our lives.

In our waiting, we don't sit back and do nothing. Our waiting is active, energetic, and deliberate. We pray as we wait, responding to the stirrings of the Spirit within us and loving those closest to us. We remain hopeful as we wait, believing that Jesus will come to us and to those who walk in darkness. All this we do in the confident expectation that Jesus will meet us with his living presence.

In the meantime, we wait in the ways mentioned, heeding at all times the words of the psalmist: "Be strong, and let your heart take courage; wait for the LORD!"

### *Daily Practice*

Throughout the day, whenever you find yourself waiting—whether in line at the grocery store, in a traffic jam, in a doctor's office, or in the school pickup line—consider what waiting for the Lord means within the context of your present life.

# HOPE

### Read Colossians 1:24-29.

*To them God chose to make known how great among the*
*Gentiles are the riches of the glory of this mystery,*
*which is Christ in you, the hope of glory.*
**Colossians 1:27**

When life gets dark within and around us, we may become discouraged. The painful crises that disrupt our lives can take us to the edge of despair. The overwhelming suffering of our world mocks the claim that this season is one of goodwill and blessing, and feelings of hopelessness contaminate our thoughts.

Against this backdrop, the evergreen wreath reminds us that the season of Advent is a time of hope. The original hope was for God's Messiah to usher in God's reign on earth, heal the rift between God and humanity, and put the world right. As followers of Jesus, we believe that this hope became flesh and blood in Bethlehem. Today, he lives in us through the presence of his Spirit. Indeed, as Paul emphasizes in his letter to the Colossians, Christ in us is the hope of glory. Through him, we have already tasted God's glorious future in the present.

Advent challenges us to live in the present moment as agents of this future hope. We can begin to share this hope wherever we find despair and discouragement. We ask God to give us words that will bring light and hope to those who walk in darkness. We invite God to comfort the hurting through our own caring presence. We find ways for our everyday work to bring about common good. We beg God to reveal God's self to those who suffer.

Wonderfully, as we seek to be a sign of Advent hope for others, we discover our own lives are filled with God's fresh possibilities. As we make God known to others, we begin to realize that Christ in us is indeed the hope of glory.

### *Daily Practice*

Choose to be a person of hope today. Think of a way you can bring hope to someone who is discouraged. After you have acted on this intention, reflect on the effects of this hope-giving action on your own life.

# JOSEPH

## Read Matthew 1:18-25.

*When Joseph awoke from sleep, he did as the angel
of the Lord commanded him.*
**Matthew 1:24**

Joseph represents the guided life. When we meet him for the first time, he is facing a painful dilemma. He is a man in love, engaged to Mary and looking forward to their wedding day. Then, he discovers that she is pregnant. He knows he is not the father because they are not yet married. This news plunges him into crisis. Nonetheless, in the midst of this upheaval, he knows what he needs to do. But how does he arrive at this clarity?

First, he courageously faces the facts in front of him. His fiancée is pregnant. He can remain with her, or he can make plans to leave her. Though he initially leans towards the latter option, he does not act impulsively. He takes time to think through his options. Joseph shows courage by considering a difficult situation from different perspectives. When we find ourselves faced with difficult decisions, we too need to reflect on them from all possible angles.

Second, Joseph listens for the word of the Lord, which comes to him in a dream. Today, God continues to speak in many ways. We experience the divine voice in creation, in the wise words of a trusted friend, in liturgy, in silent reflection, and in the words of scripture. The Bible points us toward the Living Word, Jesus Christ incarnate. Like Joseph, we need to continually listen to what God may be saying to us when we are wrestling with decision-making. Listening for the Lord lies at the heart of the guided life.

Third, Joseph follows the guidance he receives. Even though his decision could mean losing his reputation as a righteous man, he acts on the guidance he receives from God. Likewise, if we want to follow where God's Spirit leads, we need to be willing to act. If considering our possible decisions, praying about them, and attempting to listen to God points us down a particular path, we must take the first step.

Even though the Gospel of Matthew records no spoken words from Joseph concerning his decision, his life speaks loudly about the importance of finding and seeking the Lord's will. God has good purposes for every one of us. Despite the risks, genuinely seeking God's guidance remains the most important way of living in tune with what God wants for our lives. In this regard, Joseph is a wonderful mentor and friend.

### *Daily Practice*

Think about a particular decision you are facing right now. Sit down with a notepad or with your computer, and list the different options before you. Reflect on them in prayer, asking God to guide you in the days ahead.

# PATIENCE

### Read 2 Peter 3:11-18.

*Therefore, beloved, while you are waiting for these things, strive to be found by him at peace, without spot or blemish; and regard the patience of our Lord as salvation.*
**2 Peter 3:14-15**

God never seems to be in a hurry. In scripture, we see God's people waiting for centuries for the coming of the promised Messiah. As we wait for God's promises to be fulfilled in the final coming of Christ, we need to remember this. And, as today's reading suggests, God's unhurriedness is also something for which we need to be grateful because we have been given time to repent of our misdeeds and to spread the good news of Jesus to others. Indeed, as we read in Second Peter, the patience of the Lord is our salvation.

Advent provides a wonderful opportunity to let some of God's unhurriedness and patience rub off on us. Patience does not come automatically or easily to most of us. We tend to be impatient with ourselves, with others around us, and especially with the difficult circumstances we face. We want our character defects transformed in an instant. We want people to respond to our demands immediately. We want difficult situations to be fixed right now. This impatience poisons us. It infects our thoughts and actions with irritation and anger, harming both ourselves and those around us.

What does it mean to be patient? The word comes from the Latin verb *patior*, which means "to suffer." To be patient is to suffer through the present moment, especially when it is not what we want it be. Having patience means living in the here and now, being fully attentive to the people and events in our lives, and being open to the seeds of growth and personal change hidden in each difficult and imperfect circumstance.

Not surprisingly, such patience is not simply the result of our willpower; it is the fruit of God's Spirit living within us. This Advent, may we cooperate with the Spirit and embrace those opportunities that teach us patience.

### *Daily Practice*

One way to cooperate with the Spirit is to practice patience in the ordinary moments of our day—choosing the longer check-out line at the store, giving more consideration to a colleague who missed a deadline, or driving the speed limit. God uses ordinary moments like these to grow the fruit of the Spirit within us.

# HIDDEN

### Read Colossians 3:1-3.

*Set your mind on things that are above, not on things that are on earth, for you have died, and your life is hidden with Christ in God.*
**Colossians 3:2-3**

In a culture obsessed with celebrity status, social media followers, and garnering recognition, Paul's invitation to live a hidden life sounds radically countercultural. We tend to resist hiding. We want to be seen as having much to offer, as being indispensable to those around us, and as being popular in the eyes of the world. While wanting to live a significant life may not be a bad desire, our resistance to being hidden can cause us to rely more on how others see us than on how God sees us.

The theme of being hidden runs through much of Jesus' life. Think of his birth in an insignificant Palestinian village far from the big cities, his character-forming years with Mary and Joseph in Nazareth about which we know so little, his behind-the-scenes formation for ministry during his teenage and young adult years, and his many hours spent in solitude and prayer during his years of ministry. He knows what it means to live a hidden life in the midst of three highly public years.

Perhaps Advent invites us to practice solitude as well. At a practical level, this simply means carving out time to be alone during the busyness of the season. Planned solitude helps us remember who we are and allows us to focus on our own spiritual formation. It reminds us that God loves us just as we are. It lessens our need for others' affirmation and approval and frees us to be more willing to act on whatever God is calling us to do. Above all, solitude prepares our hearts to receive God's love and mercy.

I've heard people say that genuine saints are always hidden. In the solitude, in the ordinary, and in the unspectacular, they work on their relationship with God in ways that others may not notice. Even so, by focusing on who God would have them be, they shine, bringing the light of God into the world. May we aspire to do the same.

### *Daily Practice*

Create a mini-Advent retreat for yourself today. Carve out a time for solitude, and focus your attention on God. Who is God calling you to be today, during this Advent season, and every day?

# REMEMBER

**Read 2 Timothy 2:8-10.**

*Remember Jesus Christ, raised from the dead, a descendant of David—that is my gospel, for which I suffer hardship, even to the point of being chained like a criminal.*
**2 Timothy 2:8-9**

Our faith is rooted in remembrance. Scholars of early church history remind us that within the early Christian communities the first obligations of disciples were teaching and helping new Christ followers develop a Christian memory. Such a memory found its primary focus in Jesus, leading Peter to encourage those to whom he wrote with the following words: "Remember Jesus Christ."

During Advent, we remember the mystery of the first Christmas. Something happened that day that had never happened before. God slips into human history in the same way that we enter the world: through a woman's womb as a crying infant who needs to be held and fed, vulnerable and dependent like all of humanity. God becomes like you and me so that we may know the way and the truth and the life. Today—and each day of Advent—we remember this.

But we don't only remember Jesus as a baby. We also remember him in his deeds and his words, in his death and his resurrection. Christmas points us to Good Friday and to Easter Sunday. The One who we remember today lives beyond death as our risen Lord and Savior, residing within and among us. He is alive, present throughout the universe, and available and accessible to each one of us. Today we remember this. The Messiah has been raised from the dead.

Developing a Christian memory is not about living in the past. We remember so that we can live with hearts open to the Christ who is alive and present with us today and every day.

### *Daily Practice*

Take some time today to remember the moment when Christ became more than a word for you. Give thanks to God for the memory, and allow it to lead you into a fresh openness toward Christ today.

# WITH

### Read Matthew 1:23-25.

*"Look, the virgin shall conceive and bear a son,*
*and they shall name him Emmanuel,"*
*which means, "God is with us."*
**Matthew 1:23**

One of my favorite versions of scripture is The Life with God Bible. The title is a powerful reminder that the Bible is all about human beings living with God. Little wonder that one of the names given to Jesus is *Emmanuel*, which means, "God is with us." What does this mean for us during Advent?

Throughout scripture, God promises again and again, "I am with you." Beginning in Genesis, we witness God's living presence with people in all the ordinary and extraordinary circumstances of their lives. Advent reminds us that God's promise became flesh and blood in Jesus Christ. Perhaps we must never again think of the world as being without God or God being distant and faraway. Throughout all our experiences and encounters, God is present with us and will be even to the end of the age.

Moreover, God's promise—"I am with you"—comes with an invitation—"Will you be with me?" *With* is a powerful word that evokes a sense of connection and partnership. God does not bulldoze over us, forcing God's self into our lives. We can choose to live without God. Adam and Eve make this decision with their devastating choice in the garden, and the consequences of their decision affect us even today. Wonderfully, even though we repeatedly turn our backs on God, Advent reminds us that God never gives up on us and continues to live within us, offering a steadfast love that will not let us go.

Advent is a time to remember both God's promise and God's invitation. Let us today hear again God saying to us in our depths, "I am with you," and may we respond by saying to God, "I want to live with you." As we listen for God's grace-filled invitation and respond to it, we will experience for ourselves the gift of the with-God life.

### *Daily Practice*

Every time you begin a new activity today at work or home, say to God, "I want to do this with you." Expect God to work with you and through you in everything you do.

# LIGHT

### Read Isaiah 9:1-2.

*The people who walked in darkness*
*have seen a great light;*
*those who lived in a land of deep darkness—*
*on them light has shined.*
### Isaiah 9:2

Advent can be a gloomy time. Often, our hearts are filled with feelings of grief, isolation, and depression. Ironically, the celebrations of this season underline this gloominess even more. How can we break free of these difficult emotions?

Advent reminds us that the coming of the Christ child brings light into the gloom and darkness of this world. How does Jesus do this? He forgives the guilty. He delivers the oppressed. He welcomes the stranger. He comforts the grieving. He heals the sick. He plays with children. He strengthens the weak. Imagine the light! Light streams into our lives when we know we are valued, loved, and cherished by God and by others. This is what hurt, broken, and despairing people experience in Jesus' presence, and we can too.

Today, the risen Christ wants to shine his light into our gloomy existence. One of the best ways to receive his light is to share honestly with him about what is happening in our lives. As we tell him about our pain and loss, we give him access to our painful emotions. We allow his healing light to enter the darkness within us, and we remember that he is Emmanuel. We are not alone.

### *Daily Practice*

Experiment praying with your imagination today. Close your eyes, and imagine yourself sitting alone in a dark room. Envision Jesus entering the room with God's light streaming through his whole being. For a few moments, allow his light to shine on whatever gloom occupies your heart.

# JOY

### Read Luke 2:10-14.

*The angel said to [the shepherds], "Do not be afraid; for see—*
*I am bringing you good news of great joy for all the people."*
**Luke 2:10**

Some of us have difficulty opening ourselves to the joy of the Lord when we feel surrounded by suffering. We feel as though we must engage with the pain around us, but we forget to embrace the joy. We find ourselves distrustful, suspicious, and even resistant to the possibilities of experiencing the joy found in Jesus Christ.

And perhaps we have good reason for our reluctance. We have been badly hurt and let down in the past. We know that life can be terribly unfair, and maybe we struggle with a disposition that leans toward despair rather than hope. Perhaps we are scared that if we open ourselves to joy, we will face disappointment. Whatever the reason, we may find ourselves fearing joy. Little wonder that the angel, when bringing the shepherds good news of great joy, tells them not to be afraid.

Advent invites us to overcome our fear and to receive the joy that Jesus brings. Not only is he a man filled with great joy, but also he wants to share that joy with us. His joy, so evident in his life, is not blind to the presence of suffering, evil, and death. Jesus faces these realities head-on. The joy that he offers has been tested by everything that so often robs us of ours. Because of Jesus' life, crucifixion, and resurrection, we can trust that his joy is stronger than all its opponents.

What keeps us from experiencing joy? May we be willing to release our fears and allow the joy of Jesus into our hearts and minds.

### *Daily Practice*

Make a conscious effort today to rejoice in the good gifts that come your way—a warm cup of coffee, the friendly face of a loved one, the beauty of a sunrise or sunset. Receive God's gift of joy in these moments.

# THE MAGI

### Read Matthew 2:1-12.

*"Where is the child who has been born king of the Jews? For we observed his star at its rising, and have come to pay him homage."*
**Matthew 2:2**

The magi represent a life of both seeking and surrendering. While we do not know how many magi come looking for Jesus, the Gospel of Matthew does tell us a few facts. They come from the East. They come bearing gifts. Above all, we know that they seek a new ruler—a king of the Jews. As such, they speak to us in our own longing for God.

Strikingly, we see that God initiates the magi's seeking by giving them a star. Today, God continues to give us stars to help us seek a godly direction. These "stars" come with different names and in different ways, such as the star of our holy discontent that stirs up a certain restlessness within our lives, the star of our search for what is lasting, and the star of our need for meaning. These stars and others remind us that God has placed eternity in our heart, and we will never be at home until we find our true home in God.

The magi challenge us to be serious about our seeking. They leave everything to follow the star. They ask questions and receive guidance. They invest time, effort, and energy in their journey. They even risk their safety by going against Herod's wishes. By comparison, our seeking often appears lukewarm at best.

The magi's seeking leads them to the Christ child, but our own seeking often leads us to the wrong address. Instead of seeking God as the prophet Jeremiah suggests—"When you search for me, you will find me; if you seek me with all your heart" (29:13)—we allow our search for money, a perfect holiday gathering, or gifts to get in the way. The message of Christmas proclaims that God's address is Jesus Christ. Whatever route we follow, let us find our way to the right address!

In addition to seeking Jesus, the magi also surrender themselves to him. When they arrive at Mary and Joseph's house, they kneel before Jesus and offer him gifts of great value. These gifts represent their surrender. Self-surrender leads us into an experiential knowledge of Emmanuel. It gives God deeper access to our lives. Shifting from a self-centered lifestyle to a God-centered way of life requires a lifetime of surrender.

God wants to be sought. The good news is that as we intentionally seek God, God meets us in our seeking and embraces us with a great love. As we surrender ourselves each day to this love, we can give ourselves to God and to those around us in new and life-giving ways. When we strive to seek and to surrender, the miracle of Christmas can happen every day.

### *Daily Practice*

Find a few minutes to be alone. Adopt a body posture that best embodies your desire to surrender yourself to God. You may choose to sit with open or outstretched hands, to lie on the floor, to stand with hands raised, or to kneel. Express your longing for God through your body.

# PONDER

### Read Luke 1:26-38.

*But [Mary] was much perplexed by [Gabriel's] words and
pondered what sort of greeting this might be.*
**Luke 1:29**

Early in my career as a pastor, I received insight that I have not
forgotten from one of my mentors. It has shaped the way I live
and minister profoundly. As I was sitting in my mentor's office
one morning, talking about work over the past week, he said,
"Always remember, Trevor, we don't learn from experience. We
learn when we reflect on experience."

Mary, the mother of Jesus, guides us in this task of reflection. We see in Luke's Gospel that she ponders the events of her
life. In our reading today, when the angel Gabriel surprises her
with a word of greeting and tells her of God's favor, we read that
she ponders his greeting. In this small detail, we catch a glimpse
of the contemplative Mary, turning things over in her mind and
heart, wondering what they may mean for her life.

In the frantic rush of this pre-Christmas season, I see an
important learning for us. We can so easily slip into an unreflec-
tive way of living, filling our days with shopping, partying, and
finishing our work for the year without ever stopping to notice
what is happening within and around us. Little wonder that we
seldom learn from our experiences, repeat the same mistakes,
and get caught in destructive patterns of living. Only when
we stop to ponder our experiences do we extract those hidden
insights that can change our lives for the better.

### *Daily Practice*

Before going to bed, take a few minutes to ponder the events of the day. Ask God to help you discover the significant—or seemingly insignificant—occurrences that require more attention and reflection.

# HOME

### Read Luke 1:39-45, 56.

*Mary remained with [Elizabeth] about three months
and then returned to her home.*
### Luke 1:56

The demands we place upon ourselves during the Christmas season often bring much strain into our homes. Rather than being safe places of renewal, rest, and joyful connection, our homes become places of stress, argument, and conflict. Living in such an environment prohibits us from entering into the spirit of Advent.

Mary decides to visit her cousin Elizabeth, who is also unexpectedly pregnant, to help her through the difficult demands of her final three months of pregnancy. Pregnancy, especially for older parents like Elizabeth and Zechariah, can bring surprise and stress, excitement and tension, anticipation and dread. Touchingly, in Mary's caring and compassionate visit, the Christ child in Mary's womb brings both joy and the Holy Spirit into Elizabeth and Zechariah's home.

In this story, we see a striking example of what can happen when we bring the spirit of Jesus into our family relationships. We can choose to fill ours homes with joy and with a sense of God's presence—but not without thoughtful gestures of care and compassion. We show others care and compassion by being attentive to their needs, by listening thoughtfully to their troubles, by offering intentional acts of kindness, or by speaking words of apology or forgiveness for past wrongdoings. Jesus wants to change the atmosphere in our homes and families through our words and actions, but, ultimately, this task is up to us to complete.

## *Daily Practice*

Think of one practical way in which you can bring Jesus' presence into your home and your relationships. As you put your intention into practice, ask Jesus to express himself through you.

# GRACE

### Read John 1:14-18.

*From [the Word's] fullness we have all received, grace upon grace.*
**John 1:16**

*Grace* is one of those familiar biblical concepts that we sometimes rob of its meaning. We dare not allow this to happen. Advent offers us a wonderful opportunity not only to think again about the meaning grace has for our journey of faith but also to receive anew its power for our lives.

As the writer of the Gospel of John explains, in the coming of the Word, God pours additional grace into the world. Certainly grace had come through the gift of the Law to Moses, but Jesus offers something more. Hence, when the Word becomes flesh, "grace upon grace" is now available. New resources of God's loving power are within reach of ordinary people. This fuller experience of grace makes it possible for us to experience God's salvation in a way that those who lived before Jesus simply could not.

The grace of our Lord Jesus Christ does not just forgive us. The bumper sticker that says, "Christians are not perfect—just forgiven" gets it wrong. Sure, we are imperfect, but we are not merely forgiven. Grace provides a spiritual power that radically changes and transforms our lives. It enables us to accomplish what we cannot do by our own strength—that is, to become the changed people that God wants us to be. So we need all the grace we can get.

God's transforming grace will not enter our lives without our effort. Grace, as author and friend Dallas Willard would often say, is opposed to earning but not to effort. This is why we should engage in simple spiritual practices each day. They are the practical means by which we position ourselves before God so that God's grace can flow more deeply into our lives and gradually change us into the people God wants us to be.

### *Daily Practice*

Where do you struggle the most in your walk with God? Share your struggle with God, yielding to God's wisdom and asking for God's gift of grace.

# RECEIVE

### Read John 1:10-13.

*To all who received him, who believed in his name,*
*he gave power to become children of God.*
### John 1:12

How often have we heard Jesus' words, "It is more blessed to give than to receive" (Acts 20:35)? But we cannot give what we have not received. And, sadly, many of us do struggle to receive, especially when it comes to God's gift to us that we celebrate during Advent. In our struggle, we miss the greatest opportunity of the season.

During Advent, we celebrate God's indescribable gift of Jesus. He comes into the world as the way into God's own heart, the truth of who God is, the life that God gives. God offers this gift to everyone and anyone through faith. We needn't be born of a certain race, tribe, or culture. We needn't display any external credentials, marks of righteousness, or certificates of accomplishment. We all hold a unique place in God's divine family. All God asks us in return is that we receive Jesus Christ into our lives and believe in his name.

Receiving Jesus is not merely a mental exercise—it requires risk and action. When we receive Jesus, we affirm that we are loved, accepted, and forgiven unconditionally. Then, we encounter a new language—the language of self-giving and sacrificial love. As members of God's family, we discover a rich family history to make our own—a history of God's people that stretches from biblical times to the present. We have new habits to adopt—habits of worship and prayer, sharing and serving, giving and receiving. We live in a new kingdom, breathing in the atmosphere of the Spirit who transforms our hearts and minds.

Such receiving is never for our sake alone. Receiving the gifts of God's unconditional acceptance and forgiveness, as well as the gifts of a new family and a new kingdom in which the Spirit is both powerfully present and active, makes giving ourselves to others in radical ways possible. We journey from self-centeredness to other-centeredness, from greed to generosity, from hostility to hospitality. We become agents of God's new creation, and we spread the spirit of Christmas throughout the world.

### *Daily Practice*

Sit quietly with closed fists. Then, open your hands slowly as an outward expression of your intention to receive Jesus this Advent.

# REJOICE

### Read Luke 1:46-56.

*"My soul magnifies the Lord,*
*and my spirit rejoices in God my Savior."*
**Luke 1:46-47**

Our reading tells us that as soon as the angel Gabriel leaves Mary, she quickly embarks on a journey to see her cousin Elizabeth. When she enters Elizabeth's home, Elizabeth offers her a beautiful blessing. Mary responds by breaking into song, praising the Lord and rejoicing in God as her Savior.

Advent invites us to participate in a similar rejoicing. We have every reason to celebrate God during this season of the Christian calendar. Christmas reminds us that God stepped into human history to topple the powers of evil. This victory has been accomplished through the life, death, and resurrection of Jesus. The Light truly entered the world, and the darkness could not extinguish it. We too can sing songs of celebration and joy that magnify the Lord and rejoice in our Savior.

Something happens in us when we rejoice in what God has done. God's goodness and faithfulness grow bigger in our heart and mind. A new joy wells up within us, filling us with happiness. We experience a sense of well-being, even if we are experiencing dark and difficult times. Our faith deepens, our hope grows stronger, and our love for God and others expands. We feel encouraged in our walk with God, and our desire to share in God's work in the world is strengthened and empowered. In short, rejoicing radically transforms us.

When we reflect on the transformative effects of rejoicing, we can understand why Paul exhorts the early church with the following words: "Rejoice in the Lord always; again I will say, Rejoice" (Phil. 4:4). Let us rejoice with Mary, with Elizabeth, with Paul, and with the whole cloud of believers!

### *Daily Practice*

Recall one way in which God has saved you and offered you new life. Take time to rejoice in this gift of salvation by clapping your hands, dancing, singing your favorite hymn, or telling God how thankful you are.

# SIGN

### Read Luke 2:8-12.

*"This will be a sign for you: you will find a child wrapped
in bands of cloth and lying in a manger."*
**Luke 2:12**

Just after Jesus' birth, the shepherds encounter an angel who
tells them where they will find the Messiah: lying in a manger.
This would be their sign. Notice that the manger itself is nothing
special. It serves merely as a signpost, pointing to the identity of
the baby boy who is found there. Still, the manger offers us two
Advent lessons—one is an invitation, and the other is a challenge.

First, the manger offers us an invitation to show our adoration to the Christ child. As a sign, the manger points beyond
itself. Its main task is to remind us of who the baby is and what
he comes to do. Jesus, the manger tells us, is God come to us
in the flesh. His birth signifies the beginning of the decisive
confrontation between God's reign and the evil of this world.
Today, as we consider Jesus' life, death, and resurrection, the
manger invites us to worship the One born there.

Second, the manger challenges us to become signposts. Just
as the manger is a sign of the arrival of the Christ child, so our
lives need to point to the One who sent him. People may look
at the world and say they see no evidence that the Messiah has
come. The world is filled with hatred, violence, enslavement,
poverty, and prejudice. But such atrocities must be confronted
by redeemed lives. Those of us who claim Jesus as our Lord must

demonstrate through our words, deeds, worship, and work that evil indeed has been conquered.

### *Daily Practice*

Listen to a recording of "O Come, All Ye Faithful," paying special attention to the line that repeats, "O come, let us adore him." As you listen to the song, gaze at a cross, a nativity scene, a piece of art that depicts Jesus' birth, or an icon. Allow yourself to be filled with adoration and love.

# THE SHEPHERDS

## Read Luke 2:8-20.

*The shepherds returned, glorifying and praising God
for all they had heard and seen.*
### Luke 2:20

The shepherds symbolize the outsiders of our day. When Jesus is born, God sends an angel not to those in political leadership or to the religious authorities of the day or to the rich and influential but to shepherds. They are the night shift, the nobodies, the ritually unclean, preventing them from taking part in temple worship. So what does the shepherds' visit tell us about God's intention and the gospel of Jesus Christ?

Most certainly, the shepherds' visit underlines God's passionate concern for the marginalized. Think of the people with whom Jesus spends most of his time: the woman caught in the act of adultery; Zacchaeus, the tax collector; people suffering from leprosy and other ailments. To these people, Jesus wants to reveal his Father's unconditional love. Jesus even tells the Pharisees, who question him for eating with tax collectors, "For I have come to call not the righteous but sinners" (Matt. 9:13). The Christmas story reminds us that the coming of the Messiah is good news for those outside the social, economic, and political elite.

The angel in Luke's Gospel—accompanied by a multitude of heavenly hosts—does a wonderful job of singing a song of God's good news. So how do we sing this song today? The best way is to explore how to make God's love real to the outsiders where we live. We need to ask ourselves, *Who are the outsiders in our midst today? Who are those who feel excluded, ignored, and looked down upon?* Our lists should include the elderly, the mentally ill, the economically poor, the incarcerated, and the refugees. What does it mean to put into practice God's concern for those who suffer and are only met with disdain and contempt?

Moreover, is Jesus not an outsider as well? He tells us, "Just as you did it to one of the least of these who are members of my family, you did it to me" (Matt. 25:40). Jesus breaks the barriers between those who are accepted inside the church and those who are kept on the outside. He praises the meek, the lonely, and the persecuted. And he puts himself in situations where he identifies with those on the margins. Jesus' birth reminds us that God chooses to show God's self to the outsiders.

### *Daily Practice*

Make a list of persons who are considered outsiders. Think of how you can express God's compassion to at least one person on this list.

# THE MESSY MANGER

## Read Luke 2:1-7.

*[Mary] gave birth to her firstborn son and wrapped him
in bands of cloth, and laid him in a manger,
because there was no place for them in the inn.*
**Luke 2:7**

How often do our lives look neat and tidy on the outside when a peek behind the scenes reveals a different story? When we combine the messiness of our own personal struggles with the hurt and heartaches of society, we realize just how messy the world really is.

The Gospel of Luke tells us that when Jesus enters the world, he is placed in a manger because no rooms were available at the nearby inn. Jesus' birth reminds us that God does not abandon us in our mess but enters into it with us. Jesus is Emmanuel—"God with us"—in whatever mess we may be experiencing. We don't need to pretend anymore that everything is okay. Our mess is where God is and wants to be.

Mess enters our lives in different ways. Mess can come from our sinful choices and their devastating consequences. Though free will allows us to make our own choices regarding any number of issues, it does not allow us to choose the consequences for our actions. Mess also comes from the decisions made by others. How often are our lives sent into a tailspin because of the thoughtless or harsh words spoken by a friend or family member?

Mess also arrives through the overwhelming grief and sadness brought on by the loss of a loved one. As we grow older, these losses mount up, making us feel more and more alone.

Jesus wants to meet us in our mess so that he can transform us. Just as he comes to Zacchaeus in a tree and to a Samaritan woman by a well, he also wants to enter the messes and muddles of our lives to bring hope and new life. So how can Jesus meet us in our mess? We must share our mess with him, humbly asking him to join us as we learn to live as his friend and disciple. As we begin a journey with him, his Spirit gets to work in us.

As followers of Jesus, we also are challenged to meet others in their messes. We reach out to them in love as Jesus reaches out to us. We bring no words of condemnation or judgment; we don't try to "fix" anyone. Instead, we offer our presence as a source of encouragement and support. We listen attentively to their stories of poor choices, heartache, and grief. We think carefully about how we can respond in a way that offers life and hope. And we allow our words and actions to point to the One who is bigger than their messes: a God who loves them and will never give up on them.

Christmas Eve offers us an opportunity to consciously open our messy lives to Jesus and to acknowledge our mess before others. Our mess becomes our message as we explain how Jesus came to us in our desperate need and as we connect lovingly with those around us.

### *Daily Practice*

When you take your trash out, remind yourself of the good news that our mess is the place where God wants to meet us. Thank God aloud for this gift of grace.

# THE MESSIAH HAS COME!

**Read Luke 2:8-20.**

*The angel said to [the shepherds], "Do not be afraid; for see—*
*I am bringing you good news of great joy for all the people:*
*to you is born this day in the city of David a Savior,*
*who is the Messiah, the Lord."*
**Luke 2:10-11**

We celebrate the wonderful news of Jesus' birth today. The Messiah has arrived! However, he turns out to be a radically different savior from the person many were expecting. People were hoping for a great warrior-king who would rebuild the Temple, liberate Israel from its Roman oppressors, and usher in a new Jewish kingdom. Instead, Jesus makes God's kingdom available to all nations, keeps company with outsiders and misfits, loves his enemies, and faces execution on a cross. Jesus' death could have signaled that he was not the Messiah, but fortunately that was not the end of Jesus' story.

Jesus' life begins in a manger, but it does not end on the cross. A Messiah who is killed and who remains dead could never claim to be God's Anointed One. On the third day after Jesus' death, God raises Jesus from the grave, vindicating the messianic claims of his earlier ministry. Today, his risen and ascended presence fills the universe and continues to be freely available to every human being. Christmas Day invites us not only to remember Jesus' birth but also to reconsider what Jesus' life, death, and resurrection mean to us.

Jesus' birth reminds us that we are not the Messiah. A breeze of a great freedom blows into our lives when we acknowledge this. We can give up "playing God," stop trying to fix ourselves, and put an end to our futile attempts to change those around us. We also can let go of our expectations that earthly leaders will bring us salvation. While they may certainly make changes in our society—for better or for worse—politics alone cannot bring about a world that fully satisfies the eternal longings of the human heart for peace, joy, and freedom.

This does not mean that we should sit back, sing Christmas carols, and do nothing. Because the Messiah has come, we are invited to trust him. Through his life, death, and resurrection, Jesus decisively conquers the powers of sin and death. His Spirit alone can change the human heart and show us the way to create a full and flourishing life. His values of self-sacrifice, loving his neighbor, and generous hospitality are essential to our survival on this planet. His community followers consists of flawed and fallible people who are learning to love God and neighbor, learning to overcome evil with good, and learning to care for our would. All around us, usually in hidden and unheralded ways, we see this community at work, and we are invited to become part of it.

So how do we join this community? Simply by responding to Jesus' gospel invitation to "Follow me." Discipleship is not primarily about getting our doctrine right, about the decisions we make, or about having a regular quiet time. Rather, it is about keeping company with Jesus each day, getting to know him, listening to him, learning to embody his values, and being in the presence of those whose company he seeks as well.

Most importantly, to keep company with Jesus means sharing in a local community of faith. Being with Jesus always means being in community with others. We come together with others to worship, to break bread, to encourage one another in discipleship, to learn from and teach one another, to pray and serve, and to explore ways of making God's love real in the world around us. Hopefully, our life together will cause others to say, "The Messiah has truly come!"

### *Daily Practice*

Make a commitment to join a local community of faith for worship either on Christmas Day or the following Sunday.

# JOHN THE BAPTIST

**Read Matthew 3:1-12.**

*"I baptize you with water for repentance, but one*
*who is more powerful than I is coming after me . . . .*
*He will baptize you with the Holy Spirit and fire."*
**Matthew 3:11**

Even though our first impressions of John the Baptist are a bit scary, I find him to be intriguing. Dressed in camel's hair with a leather belt around his waist, John the Baptist eats locusts and wild honey. He wanders in lonely desert spaces and preaches an uncompromising message about laying an ax to the root of the tree; he even calls his audience a brood of snakes. He plunges people into the Jordan River as a sign of their repentance. But behind his austere garb, rigorous diet, harsh locale, and radical message, we see his self-effacing humility, making him the divinely chosen prophet through whom the Messiah is revealed.

How do we practice this kind of humility so that Jesus' presence may shine through our lives? As soon as we think we are making progress on the path toward humility, we become self-righteous and proud. We start to think that those around us are not quite as humble as they should be. We compare ourselves to others and think that we are more humble than they are. Before we realize it, we find ourselves in a place far removed from where we set out to be. So what can we learn from John the Baptist about genuine humility?

First, John speaks unashamedly and without pretense about the One who would be coming after him. He possesses a clear sense of his secondary role in God's salvation story. He knows he has a voice, but he is not the Word. His actions present us with a challenge. At an early age, we learn to carry ourselves in certain ways to get what we want. We manipulate the truth about ourselves in order to look more important than we really are. We give the impression that we are essential in certain situations even when we aren't. We step onto the path of genuine humility when we give up these attempts at pretending and show our true selves.

Second, John seeks to serve those around him. He does so through the message he preaches and the baptisms he performs. Humility grows in our lives as we discipline ourselves to serve others quietly and without expecting fanfare. Opportunities to act with humility present themselves every day. We can offer a ride on a rainy day to a colleague who usually walks. We can take an interest in someone who cannot enhance our reputation. We can take out the garbage without being asked. Small acts of service like these go a long way in training our habits so that we no longer act out of self-importance and pride.

Third, and most importantly, John consistently points others toward the Messiah and away from himself. John informs his followers that he can only baptize with water; Jesus will baptize with the Holy Spirit and fire. John does not seek to grab the limelight. He willingly puts himself second so that Jesus can come first. This is not always easy for us. We want to be known, to be recognized, and to feel important. When we take center stage, either in our own lives or in the lives of others, Jesus' light grows dim, and our lives fail to reveal him to those around us.

Epiphany invites us to get to know John the Baptist. As we allow him to mentor us along the path toward genuine humility, Jesus' light will begin to shine more brightly through us and into the world.

### *Daily Practice*

Experiment with John the Baptist's recipe for humility. For twenty-four hours, seek authenticity by avoiding pretense and eschewing the limelight. At the end of your experiment, reflect on your experiences and ask God for guidance.